ENGLISH PHRASAL VERBS BOOK 5

3 WORDS A DAY

KEITH S. FOLSE

KELLY SIPPELL

WAYZGOOSE PRESS

English Phrasal Verbs Book 5. 3 Words a Day

Keith S. Folse, Ph.D., Kelly Sippell

Copyright © 2025 Keith S. Folse

All rights reserved.

No part of this book may be reproduced in any form or by any electronic or mechanical means, including information storage and retrieval systems, without written permission from the author, except for the use of brief quotations in a book review.

Legal Disclaimer: All company names and websites mentioned in this book are trademarks or copyrights of their respective owners. The author is not affiliated with them in any way and does not endorse them or their ideas.

Edited by Dorothy Zemach

Cover design by getcovers.com

ISBN: 978-1961953307

Printed in the United States

CONTENTS

List of Verbs   v

Introduction   ix

Lesson 1   1
fill out; move up; sit back

Lesson 2   11
get on; rule out; take down

Lesson 3   21
give back; hand over; pick out

Lesson 4   31
come off; move out; sum up

Lesson 5   41
pass on; set down; take in

Lesson 6   52
come through; follow up; sort out

Lesson 7   62
come around; fill in; settle down

Lesson 8   72
break off; give out; go along

Lesson 9   82
come about; give in; put off

Lesson 10   92
close down; put in; set about

About the Publisher   103

LIST OF VERBS

LIST OF PHRASAL VERBS IN BOOK 5 (BY LESSON)

Lesson 1: fill out; move up; sit back

Lesson 2: get on; rule out; take down

Lesson 3: give back; hand over; pick out

Lesson 4: come off; move out; sum up

Lesson 5: pass on; set down; take in

Lesson 6: come through; follow up; sort out

Lesson 7: come around; fill in; settle down

Lesson 8: break off; give out; go along

Lesson 9: come about; give in; put off

Lesson 10: close down; put in; set about

PHRASAL VERBS IN BOOK 5 (ALPHABETICAL)

Lesson numbers in parentheses represent the first use of a phrasal verb: (2)

Lesson numbers in brackets represent a recycled phrasal verb: [10]

break off (8)

close down (10)

come about (9)

come around (7)

come off (4)

come through (6) [9]

fill in (7)

fill out (1) [6, 9]

follow up (6) [7]

get on (2) [4]

give back (3) [5]

give in (9)

give out (8) [10]

go along (8)

hand over (3) [4, 5, 7]

move out (4) [5, 6]

move up (1) [2, 3]

pass on (5) [6]

pick out (3) [4]

put in (10)

put off (9)

rule out (2)

set about (10)

set down (5)

settle down (7) [8, 9]

sit back (1) [2, 4]

sort out (6) [8]

sum up (4) [8]

take down (2) [10]

take in (5) [10]

INTRODUCTION

Phrasal verbs are one of the most difficult parts of English. They cause headaches for English learners no matter what your first language is. This book will help you with the phrasal verbs that are most frequent in spoken English.

To function well in a new language, you need vocabulary—and lots of it! Some studies say you can do simple things with just 1,000 words, but you can't really speak any language with just 1,000 words. Other experts have said you need 5,000 words, and some recent studies now say you need 10,000 (or even more!) words to speak your new language well. The more vocabulary you have in a new language, the better your speaking and listening will be.

A **phrasal verb** is one type of vocabulary. It consists of a verb and a preposition. The verb is usually a very simple short word like *get, make,* or *take.* The most common prepositions in phrasal verbs (in order of frequency) include *out, in, up, down, on, off, back,* and *over* (Gardner and Davies, 2007).

The problem for English learners is that these two words together have **a new meaning that is not the same as the meaning of just the verb or the meaning of just the preposition.** If you know the meaning of the verb and the meaning of the preposition, it does not mean you know the meaning of the phrasal verb. The meanings are often very different.

For example, let's look at the phrasal verb *call off. Call* mostly means to contact someone on the phone, and *off* is the opposite of *on.* But *call off* means *cancel* and has no connection to a phone: *The coach called off the game.* Other examples include *figure out, go on,* and *show up.*

Learning phrasal verbs is very difficult. English has hundreds of phrasal verbs, and each phrasal verb can have several meanings. In fact, frequently used phrasal verbs can have more than five different meanings.

WHY ARE THE 150 PHRASAL VERBS IN THIS BOOK IMPORTANT?

You can easily find a list of phrasal verbs on the internet, but those are just lists taken from big dictionaries. Many of those phrasal verbs are not so common, which makes them a waste of your time, and your time is important.

In these five books about phrasal verbs, you will practice the 150 most frequently used phrasal verbs in English. This list is the result of an extensive computer analysis of a large collection of approximately 130 million words of spoken English (PHaVE List: Garnier and Schmitt, 2015).

Sometimes one phrasal verb can have five or more meanings, so what should you learn first? You should learn the most common meanings, so the books in this series teach only the top meanings of each phrasal verb based on important information from a very detailed study by Liu and Myers (2020). The meanings are listed **in order of frequency**, so the first meaning is more frequently used than the second meaning, etc. (A few changes from the original list have been made for better learning.)

In sum, these books teach the most common phrasal verbs with the most common meanings in spoken English. Information about the 150 verbs chosen for these books comes from these sources:

Adolphs, Svenja, and Dawn Knight. "Building a spoken corpus." *The Routledge handbook of corpus linguistics* (2010): 38–52.

Davies, Mark. *The corpus of contemporary American English (COCA).* (2008-): available online at https://www.english-corpora.org/coca/.

Gardner, Dee, and Mark Davies. "Pointing out frequent phrasal verbs: A corpus-based analysis." *TESOL Quarterly*, 41.2 (2007): 339–359.

Garnier, Mélodie, and Norbert Schmitt. "The PHaVE List: A pedagogical list of phrasal verbs and their most frequent meaning senses." *Language Teaching Research* 19.6 (2015): 645–666.

Garnier, Mélodie, and Norbert Schmitt. "Picking up polysemous phrasal verbs: How many do learners know and what facilitates this knowledge?" *System* 59 (2016): 29–44.

Liu, Dilin. "The most frequently used English phrasal verbs in American and British English: A multicorpus examination." *TESOL Quarterly* 45.4 (2011): 661–688.

Liu, Dilin, and Daniel Myers. "The most-common phrasal verbs with their key meanings for spoken and academic written English: A corpus analysis." *Language Teaching Research* 24.3 (2020): 403–424.

HOW ARE THESE BOOKS ORGANIZED?

There are five books. The phrasal verbs in Book 1 are more common than those in Book 2, etc., so you should start with Book 1 and continue through the books in order: 2, 3, 4, 5. The order is based on an analysis of millions of words of real English.

Each book has 10 lessons. Each lesson has 3 phrasal verbs. That lesson will focus on those 3 phrasal verbs, but it will also review some of the phrasal verbs from earlier lessons, so you should also do the lessons in order.

Each lesson has these **6 practice activities**:

- Activity 1: CONVERSATION PRACTICE
- Activity 2: LEARNING NEW PHRASAL VERBS
- Activity 3: PRACTICING IMPORTANT PHRASES
- Activity 4: USING CORRECT PREPOSITIONS
- Activity 5: VERBS IN CONTEXT

- Activity 6: ONLINE PRACTICE (with a link allowing for 5 different kinds of online practice, including one for instruction)

PRACTICAL ADVICE FOR LEARNING VOCABULARY

You need a lot of vocabulary, and no one can learn this vocabulary for you. A good teacher and a good book can help, but in the end, it's all up to you.

To get more vocabulary, you need to read things in English that interest you. You need to practice speaking in English. You should try to find a conversation partner who can help you practice your lessons of three English phrasal verbs.

Keep a vocabulary notebook, either a traditional paper notebook or an electronic notebook. Every time you see a new English word, write it down. Ask yourself, "Is this word important for me in my English?" If the answer is yes, then ask, "How is this word used?" If the answer is no, then skip it and keep looking for another word.

To remember a new word, look at it carefully. Ask yourself, "Is there anything different or special about the word that can help you remember it? Is the spelling unusual or new to me? Is the word really long? Does it have any double letters?"

Examples:

- VALLEY: You can remember the word *valley* because it begins with the letter V and a valley is shaped like the letter V.

- ENVELOPE: You can remember the word *envelope* because it starts with *e* and ends with *e*, and not many words in English start and end with the letter *e*.
- MUSTARD: A personal example is the word *mustard*. I like mustard a lot, so I know I need that word when I order a sandwich at a restaurant. If I don't know this word, then I should look for that word in a dictionary and then think of something to help me remember it. To do this well, I am going to imagine a big yellow **M** on top of my sandwich, representing mustard. Whenever you find a new word, try to find something that makes that word different or special to you personally.
- DOZEN: Every time you see a new word that you think is useful for your English purposes, you should stop and make a short example in your head. If the word is *dozen*, then say to yourself, "one dozen eggs, one dozen pencils, one dozen sandwiches." It's ok to practice English with yourself in your own head. This is in fact very good practice. Use the new word and then talk to yourself (silently). It can be something as simple as "I would like some mustard, please." Yes, practice English with yourself by making a short example with each new word.

10 SUGGESTIONS FOR USING THIS BOOK

1. Open the book! Do the lessons! Many students buy a new book but do not complete the book. This book has only 10 lessons, and each lesson is short. Make time to read the book.

2. Do all the exercises. Even if an exercise seems easy, do it. The more times your brain "touches" each phrasal verb, the better your English vocabulary will become.
3. Each lesson teaches you only 3 phrasal verbs, but these verbs can have several meanings. In fact, some have two meanings, but others have five. Everyone learns differently. Some people can do one lesson in one day, but most people will need a few days with each lesson, so work hard and try to learn these very common, very useful phrasal verbs.
4. When you learn a new phrasal verb, try to learn a very short phrase with the verb. For example, when you learn FIND OUT, you should learn FIND OUT THE ANSWER or FIND OUT HER PHONE NUMBER. When you learn SET UP, you should try to remember SET UP AN APPOINTMENT or SET UP A MEETING.
5. Translations are very good when you first learn a new phrasal verb, but a translation is not your final goal. Your goal is to understand and use the phrasal verb. After you have a clear translation, then make sure you do Step 4: Learn a short phrase with the verb.
6. Every time you see a new phrasal verb, immediately try to make a personal example in your head. For example, when you learn PICK UP, ask yourself, "How can I make an example with PICK UP about my life now?" Maybe you will say, "I need to PICK UP my friend at the airport tonight" or "Please PICK UP the baby." Say this example in your head. Write it down. It is much better if you practice your new

phrasal verb in your head before you try to use it in real conversation.

7. Try to use your new vocabulary in your conversations in English. If you have a conversation partner, share your list of 3 phrasal verbs from your lesson and tell your partner that the goal is to use these 3 phrasal verbs as much as possible in your conversation.
8. Do not worry about mistakes. Remember: Practice makes perfect, so practice, practice, practice!
9. This book has many examples and exercises for each phrasal verb, but some people can remember vocabulary better if they can watch a lesson about it from a teacher. One good place to find free and easy-to-access lessons about phrasal verbs is YouTube. For example, if your new phrasal verb is *call off*, just search for "phrasal verb call off" and you will find many short lesson. Some videos are better than others, so if you find a teacher you like, then for the second phrasal verb, see if that same teacher also has a YouTube video lesson about other phrasal verbs.
10. Finally, try to use phrasal verbs you learned in Book 1, Book 2, Book 3, and Book 4. The more you practice all of these verbs, the better your English will be.

Good luck learning lots of English vocabulary!

Keith S. Folse and Kelly Sippell

LESSON 1
FILL OUT; MOVE UP; SIT BACK

ACTIVITY 1: CONVERSATION PRACTICE

Applying for a job online

Read this conversation. Think about the meanings of the **3 new bold verbs**. Then answer the comprehension questions.

Yuki: Hey, Lukas, I have some good news for you.
Lukas: Really? What is it?
Yuki: There's a job available in my department for an accountant. I really think you'd be perfect for that job! And we could work together again.
Lukas: Wow. Thank you so much for letting me know! I sent out a lot of resumes last month, but I haven't heard anything from any of those companies. I've just been **sitting back** and waiting for some good news.
Yuki: I know you've been looking for a long time. The minute I saw the job listed on the website, I knew I had to tell you about it.
Lukas: Thank you. Yes, it's been very hard to find a full-time job at a company that I really want to work for.
Yuki: Well, this is a great company to work for. There are always a lot of opportunities to **move up** into better positions, too. In fact, I got a new position just about a month ago.
Lukas: Are the benefits good?
Yuki: Yes. Good health insurance, and they even paid for me to take some extra classes.
Lukas: Great! Well, I'm ready to apply. Send me the link so I can upload my resume.
Yuki: I will, but there's also an online form you need to **fill out**. I'm not sure what information it will ask for, but you'll probably need to list some professional references. Be sure to list me. It'll help to have a refer-

ence who's already working for the company and in that same department.
Lukas: Okay, thank you. I will definitely do that.
Yuki: Lukas, I'm so glad that we might work together again.
Lukas: Me too. I'll go apply right now and let you know how it goes. Thank you again for letting me know. You're really a good friend.

1. What is the main topic of this conversation?

    a. a new job for Yuki and Lukas
    b. a new job for Yuki
    c. a new job for Lukas

2. What kind of job does Lukas have now?

    a. He works as an accountant.
    b. He sells insurance.
    c. We do not know from this conversation.

3. Why is Yuki so happy to tell Lukas about the job?

    a. She wants them to work together again.
    b. She wants the company to hire the best people.
    c. She wants Lukas to help her friends.

4. What will Lukas do to apply for the job?

   a. He will only send a resume.
   b. He will only fill out something online.
   c. He will send a resume and fill out something online.

5. What advice does Yuki give Lukas about filling out the application?

   a. Yuki tells him to list her as a reference.
   b. Yuki tells him to do it as soon as possible.
   c. Yuki tells him to check the application carefully.

6. Why is Yuki's company such a good place to work?

   a. The job is a very easy and does not include extra hours.
   b. It offers good benefits and helps people move up to different jobs.
   c. Employees do not have to work on weekends.

ACTIVITY 2: LEARNING NEW PHRASAL VERBS

Read this information about 3 phrasal verbs. Study the example sentences carefully. To help learn them, read the example sentences aloud or write them on a sheet of paper or in a document.

#121: FILL OUT

121: complete a form or special document (like a job application)

- Please **fill out** this form.
- After she **filled out** the job application, she gave it to the secretary.

#122: SIT BACK

122A: sit in a comfortable position, resting against the back of a seat

- If you **sit back** in this chair, you'll probably fall asleep.
- On the flight, I just **sat back** and watched a movie.

122B: allow something to happen by intentionally taking no action to change it

- After you put the chicken in the oven, just **sit back** for an hour until it's cooked.
- After months of planning, it was time for them to **sit back** and enjoy the trip.

#123: MOVE UP

123A: change to a better position, usually in some kind of list or ranking

- After today's match, Germany may **move up** to number one.
- The band's new song has **moved up** on this week's Top 20 List.

123B: change to an earlier date or time

- They will **move up** our meeting from the 28th to the 21st.
- The airline **moved** my flight **up** from 11:45 am to 11:30 am.

∽

ACTIVITY 3: PRACTICING IMPORTANT PHRASES

Give the phrasal verb for the meaning. Be sure to use the correct verb tense.

1. complete a form = _____ _____ a form
2. relax in your favorite chair and watch a movie = _____ _____ in your favorite chair and watch a movie
3. go from your current rank to first place = _____ _____ to first place
4. complete an application = _____ _____ an application
5. change the 2 pm meeting to noon = _____ _____ the 2 pm meeting to noon

∽

ACTIVITY 4: USING CORRECT PREPOSITIONS

Read the sentences carefully and add the missing prepositions for each phrasal verb.

1. When I'm on vacation, I enjoy **sitting** _____ and reading a good book.
2. Two days after Max **filled** _____ the application, he was able to take his new puppy home.
3. I'm grateful I had so many opportunities to **move** _____ in this organization.
4. After examining the woman, the doctor **moved** _____ the due date for the baby.
5. Can you help me figure out how to **fill** _____ all these tax forms?
6. Once the previews were over, the couple **sat** _____ and enjoyed the movie.

∽

ACTIVITY 5: VERBS IN CONTEXT

Use the context to select the correct verb for the sentence.

1. Lucy did so well on her tests that she (filled out, moved up, sat back) two levels in her language class.
2. It's been such a long week that I'm looking forward to (filling out, moving up, sitting back) and watching football all weekend.
3. Did you (fill out, move up, sit back) the application for a library card yet?

4. Because of Kia's new job, she and her fiancé decided to (fill out, move up, sit back) the date of the wedding by a few weeks.
5. After you apply for a job, it's hard to just (fill out, move up, sit back) and wait to hear something.

ACTIVITY 6: ONLINE PRACTICE

You can practice the phrasal verbs from this lesson at

https://bit.ly/3FjVwSj

Here you can use *Flashcards*, *Learn*, or *Match*. You can also have more guided practice with *Q-Chat* that offers *Teach me*, *Quiz me*, and *Apply my knowledge*.

Answers for Lesson 1

Activity 1

1. c
2. c
3. a
4. c
5. a
6. b

Activity 3

1. fill out
2. sit back
3. move up
4. fill out
5. move up

Activity 4

1. back
2. out
3. up
4. up
5. out
6. back

Activity 5

1. moved up
2. sitting back
3. fill out
4. move up
5. sit back

LESSON 2
GET ON; RULE OUT; TAKE DOWN

Traveling across the country by train

ACTIVITY 1: CONVERSATION PRACTICE

Read this conversation. Think about the meanings of the **3 new bold verbs**. Remember the meanings of the underlined verbs from earlier lessons. Then answer the comprehension questions.

Rabia: Emilio, would you be able to take care of my cat while I'm on my trip?
Emilio: Sure. How long are you going to be gone?
Rabia: About 10 days. I'm doing something I've always wanted to do: I'm taking a train across the country.
Emilio: How exciting! How long does it take to do that?
Rabia: I'll **get on** the train in Chicago, and it will take about three days to get to Los Angeles. I'll stay with my cousins for two days and then **get on** the train again in LA and be back in Chicago after another three days.
Emilio: You're really going to see a lot of the country on that trip!
Rabia: Yes, I'm really looking forward to sitting back and watching the mountains and rivers and cities go by.
Emilio: When are you leaving?
Rabia: I was going to do this over the summer, but because of my brother's wedding, I decided to move up the trip to next month. It also meant that I had to **rule out** going to Seattle. That was the original plan—Chicago to Seattle. But going now means I have to take

a different route to avoid snow in the mountains and possible delays.

Emilio: Okay. Are there any special instructions about taking care of the cat?

Rabia: I'll leave some notes for you, but it's mostly just giving her food and water.

Emilio: Do you need me to stay there?

Rabia: No. Just visiting her is okay. I hope you like cats because the first thing she'll want to do when you arrive is follow you around and hope you sit down so she can **get on** your lap.

Emilio: [*laughs*] I do like cats, so I'll look forward to that! I miss having a cat.

Rabia: She's a sweet cat, but when I'm away, she likes to knock things off the counters and sometimes the walls, so be ready! Maybe I'll **take down** the art on my walls before I leave, just to be safe.

Emilio: That sounds like a good idea. Well, just let me know when you're leaving. It'll be nice to take care of a cat again.

Rabia: Okay. Thank you.

Emilio: Have a great trip!

1. Why does Emilio need to take care of Rabia's cat?

   a. Rabia is attending his sister's wedding.
   b. Rabia is taking a trip.
   c. Rabia's cat likes Emilio.

2. Where will Rabia's trains go?

    a. to Los Angeles and back to Chicago
    b. to Chicago and back to Los Angeles
    c. to Seattle and back to Chicago

3. How many days will Rabia be on the trip?

    a. six
    b. eight
    c. more than ten

4. Why did Rabia decide not to go to Seattle?

    a. because of her brother's birthday party
    b. because she prefers California
    c. because of winter weather in the mountains

5. When is Rabia leaving for her trip?

    a. next month
    b. next summer
    c. next winter

6. What will Emilio do to take care of the cat?

    a. He will stay at Rabia's house.
    b. He will take the cat to his house.
    c. He will give the cat food and water.

∼

ACTIVITY 2: LEARNING NEW PHRASAL VERBS

Read this information about 3 phrasal verbs. Study the example sentences carefully. To help learn them, read the example sentences aloud or write them on a sheet of paper or in a document.

#124: GET ON

124A: enter a bus, a train, a subway, a plane, or similar transportation (except a car or taxi)

- The pilot and copilot usually **get on** the plane before the passengers.
- I **got on** the subway at noon.

124B: move to be on top of a thing

- Do you let your cat **get on** the kitchen table?
- When I **got on** the stage, I suddenly got really nervous.

#125: RULE OUT

125: remove or eliminate something as the possible cause or explanation

- I have three places in mind for my next vacation, but I think I can **rule out** Miami because I don't like the heat.

- The company has **ruled out** the possibility of hiring more workers at this time.

#126: TAKE DOWN

126: remove something that was on a wall, a website, or similar place

- My job is to **take down** the posters from the bulletin boards in this part of the building.
- All of a sudden, the company **took down** their website.

ACTIVITY 3: PRACTICING IMPORTANT PHRASES

Give the phrasal verb for the meaning. Be sure to use the correct verb tense.

1. eliminate Florida and New York for our next vacation = _____ _____ Florida and New York for our next vacation
2. remove the Halloween decorations = _____ _____ the Halloween decorations
3. the passengers entered the plane = the passengers _____ _____ the plane
4. remove a post on Instagram = _____ _____ a post on Instagram

5. I entered the bus at 6th Street = I _____ _____ the bus at 6th Street

ACTIVITY 4: USING CORRECT PREPOSITIONS

Read the sentences carefully and add the missing prepositions for each phrasal verb.

1. We **got** ____ the cruise ship just before it left the port.
2. **Taking** ____ the decorations after the high school dance takes a lot of time.
3. We need to **rule** ____ London as one of the options for our honeymoon. The hotels are just too expensive.
4. Will you be **getting** ____ a ladder to fix the ceiling fan?
5. Hector said the gate agent would not let him **get** ____ the plane.
6. The company **took** ____ the job posting before I could apply.

ACTIVITY 5: VERBS IN CONTEXT

Use the context to select the correct verb for the sentence.

1. Did you (get on, rule out, take down) the plane in time for your flight?

2. Please make sure to (get on, rule out, take down) all of the election posters the next day.
3. The coach just (got on, ruled out, took down) the star football player for the game because he is injured.
4. She (got on, ruled out, took down) everything from her walls before she painted.
5. Our dog tries to (get on, rule out, take down) the bed to sleep at night, but we don't let him.

∼

ACTIVITY 6: ONLINE PRACTICE

You can practice the phrasal verbs from this lesson at

https://bit.ly/3FlegRu

Here you can use *Flashcards, Learn,* or *Match.* You can also have more guided practice with *Q-Chat* that offers *Teach me, Quiz me,* and *Apply my knowledge.*

Answers for Lesson 2

Activity 1

1. b
2. a
3. b
4. c
5. a
6. c

Activity 3

1. rule out
2. take down
3. got on
4. took down
5. got on

Activity 4

1. on
2. down
3. out
4. on
5. on
6. down

Activity 5

1. get on
2. take down
3. ruled out
4. took down
5. get on

LESSON 3
GIVE BACK; HAND OVER; PICK OUT

Shopping at an outdoor farmer's market

ACTIVITY 1: CONVERSATION PRACTICE

Read this conversation. Think about the meanings of the **3 new bold verbs**. Remember the meanings of the underlined verbs from earlier lessons. Then answer the comprehension questions.

Hector: Who's next in line? <u>Move up</u>, please. Good morning! How may I help you?
Maria: Hi. This is my first time at the farmer's market. I can see now why everyone comes here. All these great vegetables and fruit and all the sunshine and fresh air, too! What a beautiful day to be out here!
Hector: Yes, and this market gets bigger every year.
Maria: So, I heard that you have the best tomatoes here. I'd like to buy some.
Hector: I've been growing tomatoes for many years. I'm happy that so many people come back to buy them. Will you be cooking them or eating them raw, like in a salad?
Maria: Cooking them. I've invited people over for brunch and I'm planning to make shakshuka. Do you know what that is?
Hector: Yes. I've eaten that dish. Tomato sauce with peppers and then eggs on top, right? It's really delicious.
Maria: Yes. So, I'll need two red peppers, too.
Hector: Please go ahead and **pick out** the peppers and tomatoes you'd like to buy.
Maria: Okay. I think I'm ready to **hand over** my money. Here's $20.

Hector: It looks like you've chosen some juicy tomatoes there. They'll make a very good tomato sauce.
Maria: I hope so.
Hector: Wait, let me **give** you **back** your change.
Maria: Thank you.
Hector: Is there anything else you need?
Maria: Not here. Let's see. I also need to buy some eggs, some spinach, and some fresh herbs for my shakshuka. And some fruit for dessert.
Hector: Oh, you can find all of that from other farmers here at the market. Good luck with your brunch.
Maria: Thank you!

1. Where is this conversation taking place?

    a. at an outdoor market
    b. at a grocery store
    c. We do not know from this conversation.

2. How many tomatoes is Maria going to buy?

    a. ten
    b. twelve
    c. We don't know from this conversation.

3. How did Hector know what shakshuka is? ?

    a. He's made it himself.
    b. He's eaten it before.
    c. He's heard about it.

4. What items did Maria buy from Hector?

   a. tomatoes
   b. tomatoes and peppers
   c. tomatoes, peppers, spinach, and eggs

5. For what meal is Maria cooking her dish?

   a. breakfast
   b. brunch
   c. lunch

6. How much did Maria pay for her tomatoes and peppers?

   a. $20
   b. less than $20
   c. more than $20

ACTIVITY 2: LEARNING NEW PHRASAL VERBS

Read this information about 3 phrasal verbs. Study the example sentences carefully. To help learn them, read the example sentences aloud or write them on a sheet of paper or in a document.

#127: GIVE BACK

127: return something to its original owner

- Don't forget to **give back** the key when you're finished with it.
- I **gave back** the money I found near my desk to the owner.

#128: HAND OVER

128A: give control or responsibility for something to someone

- When can a pilot **hand over** the plane to the co-pilot?
- When Mrs. Garcia retired, she **handed over** the business to her oldest child.

128B: give something valuable to someone with your own hands

- Do you have to **hand over** your credit card when you pay the bill in that restaurant?
- She **handed over** all the coins she had to the cashier.

#129: PICK OUT

129: select or choose

- It's not easy to **pick out** a name for a new baby.
- They **picked out** a gift for their uncle.

ACTIVITY 3: PRACTICING IMPORTANT PHRASES

Give the phrasal verb for the meaning. Be sure to use the correct verb tense.

1. choosing an apple from the basket = _____ _____ an apple from the basket
2. returned the book to someone = _____ _____ the book to someone
3. selected a name for the kitten = _____ _____ a name for the kitten
4. gave the baby to the nanny = _____ _____ the baby to the nanny
5. returning the bike you borrowed = _____ _____ the bike you borrowed

∽

ACTIVITY 4: USING CORRECT PREPOSITIONS

Read the sentences carefully and add the missing prepositions for each phrasal verb.

1. Before she went on vacation, the bank manager **handed** _____ the keys to the safe.
2. As soon as he got back from vacation, I **gave** him _____ his house keys.
3. Did you **pick** ___ a place to go to celebrate your birthday?

4. **Picking** _____ a Halloween costume is a big decision every year.
5. We were all surprised when he **handed** _____ the check for $1 million.
6. After they broke up, she **gave** ___ the engagement ring.

ACTIVITY 5: VERBS IN CONTEXT

Use the context to select the correct verb for the sentence.

1. Please (give back, hand over, pick out) my book when you're finished with it, okay?
2. Just (give back, hand over, pick out) any shirt you want, and I'll pay for it.
3. It's important to me to (give back, hand over, pick out) to my community, so I volunteer every Wednesday.
4. The police officer asked the driver to (give back, hand over, pick out) his keys because he couldn't drive.
5. It is important to (give back, hand over, pick out) fresh vegetables to make a really good salad.

ACTIVITY 6: ONLINE PRACTICE

You can practice the phrasal verbs from this lesson at

https://bit.ly/41vrt1a

Here you can use *Flashcards*, *Learn*, or *Match*. You can also have more guided practice with *Q-Chat* that offers *Teach me*, *Quiz me*, and *Apply my knowledge*.

Answers for Lesson 3

Activity 1

1. a
2. c
3. c
4. b
5. b
6. b

Activity 3

1. picking out
2. gave back
3. picked out
4. handed over
5. giving back

Activity 4

1. over
2. back
3. out
4. out
5. over
6. back

Activity 5

1. give back
2. picked out
3. give back
4. hand over
5. Picking out

LESSON 4
COME OFF; MOVE OUT; SUM UP

There are many things for a tourist to see in Italy.

ACTIVITY 1: CONVERSATION PRACTICE

Read this conversation. Think about the meanings of the **3 new bold verbs**. Remember the meanings of the <u>underlined verbs</u> from earlier lessons. Then answer the comprehension questions.

> **Tatiana:** Hey, Sofia, how are you?
> **Sofia:** Good! I just got back from my trip to southern Italy.
> **Tatiana:** Wow! I'm sure it was great. We're interested in going there too. Could you **sum up** some of the best things about that area?
> **Sofia:** Yes, easily! Wonderful beaches! Great weather! Amazing food!
> **Tatiana:** I'm jealous! I'd love to go sometime. What was your favorite of all the places you went?
> **Sofia:** Oh, that's hard to say. Hmm. I guess it would probably be the day we <u>got on</u> a boat and went out on the Mediterranean Sea and to the Amalfi Coast. The water was the most beautiful color of blue. And we were able to see much more of Italy by boat than we could have seen by bus.
> **Tatiana:** Where did you have the best food?
> **Sofia:** In Rome. I had the best pizza I've ever eaten there, and the best gelato!
> **Tatiana:** You're making me hungry. Where did you stay?
> **Sofia:** With my brother. He's been renting an apartment there for the past year while he finishes his degree. It wasn't the best time of year for me to be

away from work, but I needed to go before he **moved out.** He has to <u>hand over</u> the keys tomorrow, in fact. But I saved a lot of money by not having to stay in hotels all of the time.

Tatiana: I'm glad you were able to visit him and have such a good time.

Sofia: Yeah. The only negative thing that happened was one of the wheels on my suitcase **came off** at the very end of the trip—just as I got to the airport in Rome.

Tatiana: I'm sorry to hear that, but it sounds like you had a good trip.

Sofia: Yes, it was great. And I have plenty of time to get another suitcase before my next trip, which is only a few months away.

Tatiana: Really? Where are you going next?

Sofia: To Norway to see the Northern Lights. We just made the decision and <u>picked out</u> a tour to take. Because it's a tour, I won't have to plan anything. I can just <u>sit back</u> and not have to worry about all of the travel planning.

Tatiana: That sounds great! Do you know if it's possible for others to join that trip?

Sofia: I don't think it's too late. Let me find out.

Tatiana: Thanks.

Sofia: I think you and I would have a lot of fun traveling together!

1. Who went on a trip and to which country?

    a. Tatiana went to Norway.
    b. Sofia and Tatiana went to Norway.
    c. Sofia went to Italy.

2. What was Sofia's favorite part of the trip?

    a. enjoying the weather
    b. eating the gelato
    c. being on the Mediterranean Sea

3. Why did Sofia do in Rome?

    a. She stayed at a hotel with a great restaurant.
    b. She visited her brother.
    c. She saw the Northern Lights.

4. What happened to Sofia's suitcase?

    a. It was lost in Rome.
    b. A wheel came off in Rome.
    c. It was sent to Norway.

5. Why is Sofia looking forward to her next trip?

    a. She doesn't have to make the arrangements.
    b. She will save money.
    c. She will eat pizza.

6. What do the travelers want to see in Norway?

   a. the Northern Lights
   b. the Mediterranean Sea
   c. We do not know from this conversation.

ACTIVITY 2: LEARNING NEW PHRASAL VERBS

Read this information about 3 phrasal verbs. Study the example sentences carefully. To help learn them, read the example sentences aloud or write them on a sheet of paper or in a document.

#130: COME OFF

130A: become broken or no longer connected or a part of

- What happens if a wheel **comes off** while you are driving?
- The knob on the cabinet door **came off**.

130B: COME OFF AS: leave an impression in people's mind, often negative

- I don't want to **come off as** pushy, but we need to make a decision today.
- Because she **came off as** rude during the interview, she didn't get the job.

#131: MOVE OUT (OF)

131: permanently leave a place where you live or work

- A month before I **move out of** my apartment, I have to inform my landlord of my plans.
- My daughter **moved out** when she was 24 years old.

#132: SUM UP

132: summarize the most important points, facts, or ideas very briefly

- Can you **sum up** what the doctor told you?
- Would you **sum up** what we need to do before our next meeting?

ACTIVITY 3: PRACTICING IMPORTANT PHRASES

Give the phrasal verb for the meaning. Be sure to use the correct verb tense.

1. left the old house = _____ _____ _____ the old house
2. the hat left his head = the hat _____ _____ his head
3. he left us with the impression he was rude = he _____ _____ _____ rude
4. reporting in brief = _____ _____
5. disconnect from the car = _____ _____ the car

ACTIVITY 4: USING CORRECT PREPOSITIONS

Read the sentences carefully and add the missing prepositions for each phrasal verb.

1. Did your ring **come** _____ while you were washing the dishes?
2. When did you **move** everything _____ _____ the garage?
3. The last paragraph of the report **summed** _____ the rest of the document.
4. He felt his shoe **coming** _____ as he ran to catch the bus.
5. Every time we go out for dinner, he **comes** _____ _____ as cheap. He never pays!
6. **Sum** _____ for me what's happened in the game so far.

ACTIVITY 5: VERBS IN CONTEXT

Use the context to select the correct verb for the sentence.

1. In two weeks, the students will need to (come off, come off as, move out, move out of, sum up) the dorms.
2. The mayor (came off, came off as, moved out, moved out of, summed up) the new law for citizens.

3. The paint is already (coming off, coming off as, moving out, moving out of, summing up) the walls in the bathroom.
4. As soon as they broke off the engagement, he (came off, came off as, moved out, moved out of, summed up).
5. Be careful that you do not (come off, come off as, move out, move out of, sum up) rude to the new neighbors.

ACTIVITY 6: ONLINE PRACTICE

You can practice the phrasal verbs from this lesson at

https://bit.ly/41vrBha

Here you can use *Flashcards*, *Learn*, or *Match*. You can also have more guided practice with *Q-Chat* that offers *Teach me*, *Quiz me*, and *Apply my knowledge*.

Answers for Lesson 4

Activity 1

1. c
2. c
3. b
4. b
5. a
6. a

Activity 3

1. moved out of
2. came off
3. came off as
4. summing up
5. come off

Activity 4

1. off
2. out of
3. up
4. off
5. off as
6. up

Activity 5

1. move out of
2. summed up
3. coming off
4. moved out
5. come off as

LESSON 5
PASS ON; SET DOWN; TAKE IN

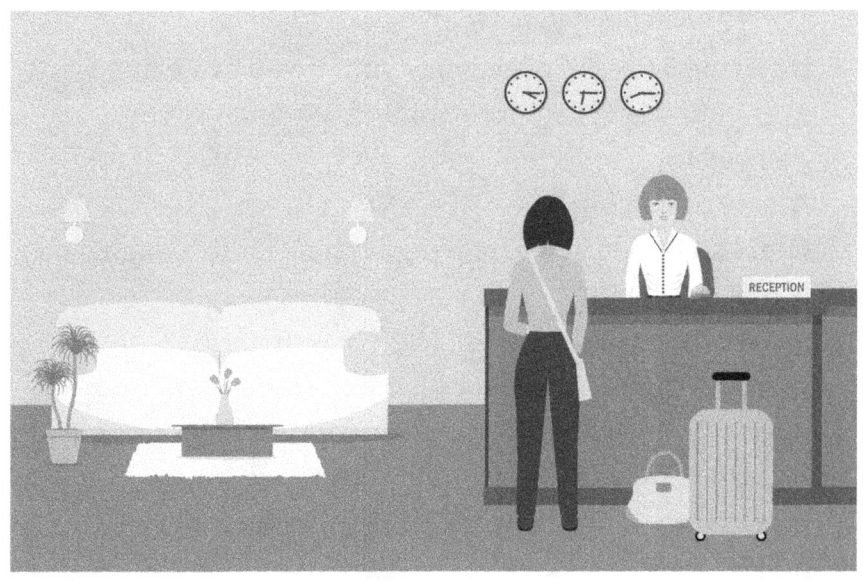

Checking into a hotel

ACTIVITY 1: CONVERSATION PRACTICE

Read this conversation. Think about the meanings of the **3 new bold verbs**. Remember the meanings of the underlined verbs from earlier lessons. Then answer the comprehension questions.

Hotel clerk: Welcome to the Jefferson hotel!
Alexis: Thank you.
Hotel clerk: Please go ahead and **set down** your bags on that cart over there, and someone can take your bags to your room.
Alexis: Okay. My last name is Romero. Is my room ready?
Hotel clerk: Yes, it's ready for you. If you can hand over your credit card for a minute, we will get you checked in.
Alexis: Here you go.
Hotel clerk: So, you're staying with us for four nights. Is that correct?
Alexis: Yes.
Hotel clerk: Is this trip for business or pleasure?
Alexis: Unfortunately, neither. My grandfather passed away, so I'm here for his funeral and to help my grandmother, who now needs to move out of her house.
Hotel clerk: Oh, I'm sorry to hear that. Here, let me give you your card back.
Alexis: Thank you.
Hotel clerk: Here's your room key and some information about the free breakfast we offer every morning

between 6 and 10 am. We also have a restaurant that serves lunch and dinner that's open until 10 pm.
Alexis: Okay. Oh, could you please ask room service to bring five bottled waters to my room?
Hotel clerk: Yes, I'll be sure to **pass on** that request to room service in just a few minutes, if you don't mind, after I take care of the next guest who's waiting just behind you. And just so you know, you can also call room service for food or drinks any time you want.
Alexis: Sure, that sounds great. Thanks again.
Hotel clerk: Despite the circumstances, I hope you'll be able to enjoy your stay here. If you're interested, we have a fitness center and a gift shop, too. Oh, and your room is in a really good location in the hotel. I hope you'll have a chance to **take in** the view of the city at night from your room. It's beautiful!
Alexis: Thanks.
Hotel clerk: And I'll have your bags sent up to your room in just a few minutes.

1. What is the first thing Alexis gives to the hotel staff?

    a. her credit card
    b. her name
    c. her business card

2. Why is Alexis visiting this area now?

    a. for business
    b. for vacation
    c. for a funeral

3. If Alexis wants to eat at the hotel at 12:00 pm, where can she get food?

   a. only at the hotel's restaurant
   b. only from room service
   c. at the hotel's restaurant or from room service

4. Which of these does the hotel provide?

   a. a restaurant that is open 24 hours
   b. a gift shop
   c. a taxi service

5. What does Alexis's hotel room have?

   a. a great view of the city at night
   b. free food in the refrigerator
   c. We do not know from this conversation.

6. What will happen to Alexis's suitcases?

   a. Alexis will carry them to her room.
   b. Someone will take them to her room.
   c. They will stay in Alexis's car.

ACTIVITY 2: LEARNING NEW PHRASAL VERBS

Read this information about 3 phrasal verbs. Study the example sentences carefully. To help learn them, read the example sentences aloud or write them on a sheet of paper or in a document.

#133: PASS ON

133A: give, especially with some kind of communication or a tradition

- Please **pass on** this message to Miguel when you see him.
- My grandmother **passed on** her love of cooking to my sister.

133B: decide not to participate in something; refuse to accept something

- She decided to **pass on** that new job offer and stay in her current job.
- Thanks, but I'm going to **pass on** dessert tonight. I'm full.

#134: SET DOWN

134A: put or place something on a surface

- She carefully **set down** the expensive vase on the table.
- Even in very windy conditions, an experienced pilot can **set down** a plane without much difficulty.

134B: establish rules, guidelines, or ideas, often in writing

- A good teacher always **sets down** the rules for the class from the first day.
- Our boss has **set down** clear guidelines for getting a raise.

#135: TAKE IN

135A: fully understand the meaning of something; appreciate the beauty of something

- It is hard to **take in** all the information in that class.
- They stood at the top of the mountain and **took in** the beautiful view.

135B: gain financially

- Can imagine how much money a large supermarket **takes in** on the weekend?
- How much does that company **take in** every quarter?

135C: provide someone with a place to stay or live, usually for a short period of time

- I **took in** my grandson when he wanted to leave home.
- When Josh lost his job last year, we **took** him **in** for a few months.

ACTIVITY 3: PRACTICING IMPORTANT PHRASES

Give the phrasal verb for the meaning. Be sure to use the correct verb tense.

1. give a message to someone = _____ _____ a message to someone
2. giving someone a temporary home = _____ _____ someone
3. place on the counter = _____ _____ on the counter
4. decide not to go camping = _____ _____ going camping
5. make a lot of money = _____ _____ a lot of money

ACTIVITY 4: USING CORRECT PREPOSITIONS

Read the sentences carefully and add the missing prepositions for each phrasal verb.

1. Why don't you **set** _____ those heavy boxes and take a break?
2. Please **pass** _____ my sympathies on to your sister. I heard her dog died.
3. Were you able to **take** _____ enough money working over the holidays to take your vacation?
4. I have a deadline, so I'm going to **pass** _____ going out tonight.

5. I'd be happy to **take** _____ your dog while you are on vacation.
6. My landlord **set** _____ clear rules about the colors you can paint your front door.

ACTIVITY 5: VERBS IN CONTEXT

Use the context to select the correct verb for the sentence.

1. How much money did that restaurant (pass on, set down, take in) last weekend?
2. My boss asked me to (pass on, set down, take in) this report to you after I finish.
3. We love the view from our hotel room. Let's just (pass it on, set it down, take it in) for a few minutes.
4. I was sorry to hear that you (passed on, set down, took in) an opportunity to work in Brazil for a year.
5. Can you (pass on, set down, take in) your coffee cup on the table and help me with these grocery bags?

ACTIVITY 6: ONLINE PRACTICE

You can practice the phrasal verbs from this lesson at

https://bit.ly/4kDLHP1

Here you can use *Flashcards*, *Learn*, or *Match*. You can also have more guided practice with *Q-Chat* that offers *Teach me, Quiz me,* and *Apply my knowledge.*

Answers for Lesson 5

Activity 1

1. b
2. c
3. c
4. b
5. a
6. b

Activity 3

1. pass on
2. taking in
3. set down
4. pass on
5. take in

Activity 4

1. down
2. on
3. in
4. on
5. in
6. down

Activity 5

1. take in
2. pass on
3. take it in
4. passed on
5. Set down

LESSON 6
COME THROUGH; FOLLOW UP; SORT OUT

Sorting and filing office papers

ACTIVITY 1: CONVERSATION PRACTICE

Read this conversation. Think about the meanings of the **3 new bold verbs**. Remember the meanings of the underlined verbs from earlier lessons. Then answer the comprehension questions.

Tanya: What are you doing?
Benji: I'm going through all these old files to try to **sort out** which ones I can throw away and which ones I need to keep.
Tanya: If it's our taxes, I think we only need to keep things for the last seven years.
Benji: Oh, that's good to know. What about other types of paperwork like bills?
Tanya: It must be less than that. Maybe three years?
Benji: Okay. I'll go with that.
Tanya: More filing space would be good.
Benji: Well, actually, I'm trying to clear out some space so I can have a better workstation at home.
Tanya: Oh, that's a good idea. I've heard you complain about space when you've had to work from home. I'm glad I can't do my job from home. We don't have space in this room for both of us.
Benji: No, we don't. I don't feel like I'm getting as much work done as I should because I only have this one laptop monitor. If I can get rid of enough paperwork, I can move this filing cabinet out, and that will create space for a second, bigger computer monitor. I'll need that if that promotion **comes through** because I'll be spending even more time filling out forms online.

That bigger monitor will really help. Do you want to help me?

Tanya: No, not really. Sorry, I'm going to <u>pass on</u> that. I hope it goes well, though! I'm going to go downstairs and finish up the laundry. I'll **follow up** with you in about an hour to see how it's going.

Benji: Okay.

1. Where does this conversation take place?

    a. at Benji's workplace
    b. in Benji and Tanya's home
    c. in an office supply store

2. What is Benji doing?

    a. organizing files and papers
    b. filling out forms
    c. laundry

3. What paperwork can they get rid of after seven years?

    a. bills
    b. taxes
    c. bills and taxes

4. What item does Benji want to move out of the room?

    a. a printer
    b. a filing cabinet
    c. a computer monitor

5. What is Benji's job?

   a. He works with spreadsheets.
   b. He fixes computers.
   c. We do not know from this conversation.

6. What do we know about Tanya's job?

   a. She helps people with their taxes.
   b. She washes clothes.
   c. Her job does not require her to work from home.

ACTIVITY 2: LEARNING NEW PHRASAL VERBS

Read this information about 3 phrasal verbs. Study the example sentences carefully. To help learn them, read the example sentences aloud or write them on a sheet of paper or in a document.

#136: COME THROUGH

136A: succeed in reaching a final destination (often used with important information or documents)

- If your visa does not **come through** by Tuesday, you cannot travel this week.
- When the email about the new director **came through,** a lot of people were happy.

136B: COME THROUGH [with something] [for someone]: provide something needed

- I'm hoping my sister will **come through** with the money I need.
- Last time we needed help, our friend Daniel **came through** for us.

#137: FOLLOW UP

137A: FOLLOW UP (WITH): take additional action about something (after something was already done) to improve the situation

- After the meeting, I'll **follow up with** a summary of the next items we should do.
- The doctor **followed up** my first treatment with two more treatments.

137B: FOLLOW UP (ON): find out additional information about something

- I don't see any changes in my account, so I am going to call the bank to **follow up on** the payment I made last week.
- I paid my bill online last week, and then I called the bank today to **follow up** and make sure they received my payment.

#138: SORT OUT

138A: get information to understand a situation better, often to solve a problem

- When the manager arrived at the restaurant, she had to **sort out** what had really happened.
- She finally **sorted out** the problem she had with a charge on her credit card.

138B: organize in a systematic way

- I need to **sort out** all these papers on my desk.
- Good luck **sorting out** all these receipts!

ACTIVITY 3: PRACTICING IMPORTANT PHRASES

Give the phrasal verb for the meaning. Be sure to use the correct verb tense.

1. provided needed food = ____ ____ ____ food
2. determined who was responsible = ____ ____ who was responsible
3. paperwork arrived in time = paperwork ____ ____ in time
4. taking additional action on = ____ ____ ____
5. organizing the bills = ____ ____ the bills

ACTIVITY 4: USING CORRECT PREPOSITIONS

Read the sentences carefully and add the missing prepositions for each phrasal verb.

1. Did that important email message **come** _____ yet?
2. This is an appointment to **follow** _____ _____ your progress since the surgery.
3. Could we **sort** _____ who will pick up the kids from school this week?
4. Did everything get **sorted** _____ at the bank yesterday?
5. Thanks for **coming** _____ for me last week at work while I was out sick.
6. I'm just **following** _____ _____ you: Did you send that check yet?

ACTIVITY 5: VERBS IN CONTEXT

Use the context to select the correct verb for the sentence.

1. Do you think the police will be able to (come through, follow up, follow up with, sort out) who stole the money?
2. My neighbors really (came through, followed up, followed up with, sorted out) after our basement flooded.

3. I'm glad the lawyers were able to (come through, follow up, follow up with, sort out) all of the paperwork to close our business.
4. (Coming through, Following up, Following up with, Sorting out) a short email after your interview is a really good idea.
5. (Coming through, Following up, Following up with, Sorting out) which lid goes with which pot takes me too much time.

ACTIVITY 6: ONLINE PRACTICE

You can practice the phrasal verbs from this lesson at

https://bit.ly/4bGVU9r

Here you can use *Flashcards*, *Learn*, or *Match*. You can also have more guided practice with *Q-Chat* that offers *Teach me*, *Quiz me*, and *Apply my knowledge*.

Answers for Lesson 6

Activity 1

1. c
2. a
3. c
4. b
5. a
6. c

Activity 3

1. came through
2. sorted out
3. came through
4. following up on
5. sorting out

Activity 4

1. through
2. up on
3. out
4. out
5. through
6. up with

Activity 5

1. sort out
2. came through
3. sort out
4. Following up with
5. Sorting out

LESSON 7
COME AROUND; FILL IN; SETTLE DOWN

Taking care of a new baby

ACTIVITY 1: CONVERSATION PRACTICE

Read this conversation. Think about the meanings of the **3 new bold verbs**. Remember the meanings of the underlined verbs from earlier lessons. Then answer the comprehension questions.

Rachel: Hey, welcome back! You're already back at work! How was your time away from the office?
Juan: Hi. It was good. It was nice to spend time with the new baby, but I'm also happy to be back to work. I missed everything here—the work and the people. Plus, if I'm at home all day, I have to change a lot of diapers. Thanks again for **filling in** for me.
Rachel: No problem. I hope that everything is good with the baby.
Juan: Yes, she's doing well. Of course, my wife and I haven't had enough sleep, but we're **coming around to** the idea that that isn't going to happen right now. Someday, we'll be able to sleep through the night again.
Rachel: Yeah, I remember all too well what it was like when our son was a baby. You'll get through it. Just try to sleep when the baby sleeps.
Juan: We tried that, sometimes with success. But now that I'm back to work, I don't think that will work. [*laughs*]
Rachel: That's true. [*laughs*]
Juan: How did everything go here?
Rachel: Fine. It was a challenge at first since it was the end of the financial year, and there were a lot of reports

we had to create. But Kevin and Anna helped me. I didn't realize that your job required you to create and submit so many reports.

Juan: Usually it doesn't, but, yeah, at this time of year it does. I hope it wasn't too much for you in addition to your own responsibilities.

Rachel: I managed it all okay. Things **settled down** once I finished all those reports.

Juan: Good. I look forward to reading the reports and having you **fill** me **in** on the accounts that didn't meet the sales goals.

Rachel: Sounds good. I'm very happy to be <u>handing</u> those accounts <u>over</u> to you again. Give me a few hours and I'll stop by and <u>follow up</u> on all this with you.

Juan: Great! See you later.

1. Why did Rachel fill in for Juan?

    a. Juan had too many reports to produce.
    b. Juan was taking care of a new baby.
    c. Rachel wanted more work to do.

2. Why is Juan happy to be back at work?

    a. He has been sleeping well.
    b. He doesn't have to write any reports.
    c. He missed his work and the people at the office.

3. What is the baby's name?

a. Kevin
b. Anna
c. We do not know from this conversation.

4. What did Rachel do for Juan?

   a. She created reports for the end of the financial year.
   b. She created new sales accounts
   c. She changed the baby's diapers.

5. When is the end of the company's financial year?

   a. June 30
   b. December 31
   c. We do not know from this conversation.

6. When will Juan start doing his job again?

   a. in a few hours
   b. the next day
   c. He is already doing his job again.

ACTIVITY 2: LEARNING NEW PHRASAL VERBS

Read this information about 3 phrasal verbs. Study the example sentences carefully. To help learn them, read the example sentences aloud or write them on a sheet of paper or in a document.

#139: COME AROUND

139A: COME AROUND (TO): change your mind or opinion about something, usually in a positive way

- It took me some time to **come around to** her new idea for the company.
- At first, Matt was against that idea, but now he's **come around** and really likes it.

139B: arrive or come near

- If you have time later, why don't you **come around** for coffee?
- There is a cat that always **comes around** to our house at night.

139C: become available or appear (often a recurring event)

- When spring **comes around**, the snow melts and the rivers flood.
- This kind of opportunity doesn't **come around** very often, so I think you should take the new job.

#140: FILL IN

140A: add information that is missing

- The first part of the final exam in our Chinese class was multiple choice, but the second part required us to **fill in** the answers in Chinese.

- Your form has a problem. You didn't **fill in** your email or phone number.

140B: FILL IN (FOR): take someone's place at their job or in a similar situation temporarily because they are not able to do the work

- When the president is unable to do something, the vice president may **fill in**.
- Hey, I'm too sick to go to work today. Can you **fill in for** me?

#141: SETTLE DOWN

141A: become quieter or more calm

- What are some ways to get kindergarteners to **settle down** quickly?
- As soon as the teacher came in the room, the students **settled down**.

141B: begin a stable, routine, or permanent life, often in one place or with one person

- Jelena has lived in seven different cities, but we think she's finally ready to **settle down**.
- When Kevin turned 36, he finally **settled down** and bought a house in Greenville.

ACTIVITY 3: PRACTICING IMPORTANT PHRASES

Give the phrasal verb for the meaning. Be sure to use the correct verb tense.

1. begin a new life in a new city = _____ _____ in a new city
2. took someone's place = _____ _____ _____ someone
3. arrive every afternoon to visit = _____ _____ to visit
4. added information on the form = _____ _____ the form
5. becoming quiet at night = _____ _____ at night

~

ACTIVITY 4: USING CORRECT PREPOSITIONS

Read the sentences carefully and add the missing prepositions for each phrasal verb.

1. I'm glad she **came** _____ and joined us on the trip after all.
2. Do you think you can **fill** _____ for me at the pool tomorrow?
3. Were you able to get the kids **settled** _____ to take a nap?
4. Be sure to **fill** _____ all of the circles on the exam sheet correctly.
5. When they heard the ice cream truck **coming** _____, they ran into the street.

6. I think it's time for us to get married and **settle** _____.

ACTIVITY 5: VERBS IN CONTEXT

Use the context to select the correct verb for the sentence.

1. She was happy he (came around to, filled in, settled down) her idea of going to Hawaii for their honeymoon.
2. Do you know who is going to (come around, fill in, settle down) for me at work tomorrow?
3. Don't worry! Things will (come around, fill in, settle down) after the election.
4. Jill enjoys (coming around, filling in, settling down) at the thrift shop.
5. When spring (comes around, fills in, settles down), more birds come to my garden.

ACTIVITY 6: ONLINE PRACTICE

You can practice the phrasal verbs from this lesson at

https://bit.ly/3DuaGUp

Here you can use *Flashcards*, *Learn*, or *Match*. You can also have more guided practice with *Q-Chat* that offers *Teach me*, *Quiz me*, and *Apply my knowledge*.

Answers for Lesson 7

Activity 1

1. b
2. c
3. a
4. a
5. c
6. c

Activity 3

1. settle down
2. filled in for
3. come around
4. filled in
5. settling down

Activity 4

1. around
2. in
3. down
4. in
5. around
6. down

Activity 5

1. come around to
2. fill in
3. settle down
4. filling in
5. comes around

LESSON 8
BREAK OFF; GIVE OUT; GO ALONG

A bike lane on a city street

ACTIVITY 1: CONVERSATION PRACTICE

Read this conversation. Think about the meanings of the **3 new bold verbs**. Remember the meanings of the <u>underlined verbs</u> from earlier lessons. Then answer the comprehension questions.

> **Johanna:** What happened at the town council meeting last night?
> **Heather:** Well, it started off with a problem because of the weather.
> **Johanna:** The weather? What do you mean?
> **Heather:** Well, it was raining pretty hard, so the meeting started late. And between 6:30 and 7:00, it got really windy, too.
> **Johanna:** Oh. I didn't even notice that.
> **Heather:** Yeah, so we didn't start the meeting until 7:30 because the mayor and some other council members were late. And when the mayor came in, he **gave out** a new packet of material for a new item on the agenda. That's when the trouble started.
> **Johanna:** What happened? Can you <u>sum it up</u> for me?
> **Heather:** He introduced a plan to create more bike lanes to encourage people to use bicycles when they go to work. This would also help cut down on traffic.
> **Johanna:** Well, that sounds good. Why wouldn't everyone **go along** with that?
> **Heather:** Well, first, the proposal was very long, and it took us a long time to <u>sort out</u> what was included. Then we realized there was something in the proposal

that would actually make traffic worse, especially on some of the busiest streets in the city.

Johanna: Isn't there a way to do both?

Heather: There should be, but not in the current proposal. The money to create the bike lanes is connected to a special government program that requires the city to include the roads with the most traffic.

Johanna: Oh, of course.

Heather: In a perfect world, we could get the money but be able to decide ourselves which roads to add the bike lanes to. There are some places where the traffic is so heavy that reducing the number of car lanes to add the bike lanes would actually make things much worse.

Johanna: Did you vote on the new proposal?

Heather: It never got that far. There was so much conflict and anger that both sides decided to **break off** discussion for now and that the issue would be discussed again at next month's meeting. Then things settled down, and we were able to make some decisions on a few other items on the agenda.

Johanna: I'm glad it ended on a positive note.

1. What type of meeting are they discussing?

   a. a meeting about a neighborhood
   b. a meeting about the weather
   c. a meeting about a city

2. Why did the meeting start late?

a. Traffic was bad.
   b. The weather was bad.
   c. A new plan was given out.

3. The new proposal was about what?

   a. adding bike lanes
   b. removing bike lanes
   c. increasing taxes

4. Who was in favor of the new proposal?

   a. the mayor
   b. the mayor and some of the council members
   c. no one

5. What are the problems with the proposed bike lanes?

   a. They are too expensive.
   b. They will make traffic worse in some places, not better.
   c. They are not good for the environment.

6. What happened at the end of the meeting?

   a. The meeting ended early because of the weather.
   b. Everything was delayed until next month.
   c. Some items on the agenda were passed.

ACTIVITY 2: LEARNING NEW PHRASAL VERBS

Read this information about 3 phrasal verbs. Study the example sentences carefully. To help learn them, read the example sentences aloud or write them on a sheet of paper or in a document.

#142. BREAK OFF

142A: end something

- They decided to **break off** their relationship.
- The two countries **broke off** official communication because of the war.

142B: physically separate

- If a branch **breaks off** that tree, it might fall on your car.
- She **broke off** a piece of chocolate and gave it to me.

#143. GIVE OUT

143A: distribute

- At the football game, they were **giving out** free bottles of water.
- None of the TV stations **gave out** the correct location of the bank robbery.

143B: stop working or fail to work

- If my phone battery **gives out** again, it might be time to replace it.
- My printer is really old, and I'm afraid it's ready to **give out**.

#144. GO ALONG

144A: progress or develop

- Everything was **going along** fine until it started to rain.
- If construction **goes along** as we planned, the bridge will be finished in 14 more months.

144B: GO ALONG (WITH): support or agree with something

- I can't **go along with** your idea to buy Lila a new cell phone for her birthday.
- Many employees didn't like the company's new plan, but they **went along** because they were afraid they'd lose their jobs.

144C: GO ALONG (WITH): accompany

- John is driving to the mountains tomorrow, and Susana wants to go along.
- Sometimes I **go along** with my neighbor when she goes for a walk at 7 am.

ACTIVITY 3: PRACTICING IMPORTANT PHRASES

Give the phrasal verb for the meaning. Be sure to use the correct verb tense.

1. progressing as planned = ____ ____ as planned
2. handed out the candy = ____ ____ the candy
3. ended a relationship = ____ ____ a relationship
4. agreed with the new policy = ____ ____ ____ the new policy
5. separates from the tree = ____ ____ from the tree

∼

ACTIVITY 4: USING CORRECT PREPOSITIONS

Read the sentences carefully and add the missing prepositions for each phrasal verb.

1. I don't know why my knee sometimes **gives** ____ on me.
2. When Steve went to the beach, did you **go** ____?
3. How did the leg on the table **break** ___?
4. The company **gave** ____ bonuses for the holidays this year.
5. All but one of the new council members **went** ____ with the new tax proposal.
6. Do you know why your girlfriend **broke** ____ the engagement?

ACTIVITY 5: VERBS IN CONTEXT

Use the context to select the correct verb for the sentence.

1. Too many branches (broke off, gave out, went along, went along with) during the storm last night.
2. Everything was (breaking off, giving out, going along, going along with) fine until the power went out.
3. Unfortunately, the two companies decided it was best to (break off, give out, go along, go along with) their partnership.
4. I decided to (break off, give out, go along, go along with) everyone and get ice cream.
5. Would you like to (break off, give out, go along, go along with) the awards to the winners this year?

ACTIVITY 6: ONLINE PRACTICE

You can practice the phrasal verbs from this lesson at

https://bit.ly/41vrYs4

Here you can use *Flashcards*, *Learn*, or *Match*. You can also have more guided practice with *Q-Chat* that offers *Teach me*, *Quiz me*, and *Apply my knowledge*.

Answers for Lesson 8

Activity 1

1. c
2. b
3. a
4. b
5. b
6. c

Activity 3

1. going along
2. gave out
3. broke off
4. went along with
5. breaks off

Activity 4

1. out
2. along
3. off
4. out
5. along
6. off

Activity 5

1. broke off
2. going along
3. break off
4. go along with
5. give out

LESSON 9

COME ABOUT; GIVE IN; PUT OFF

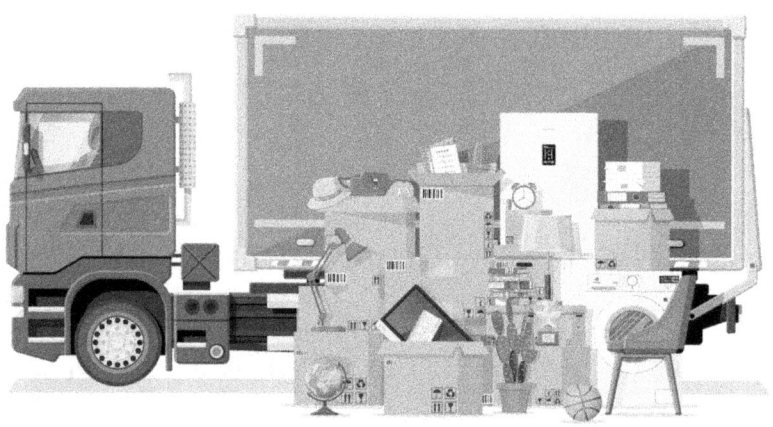

Moving to a new house

ACTIVITY 1: CONVERSATION PRACTICE

Read this conversation. Think about the meanings of the **3 new bold verbs**. Remember the meanings of the <u>underlined</u>

<u>verbs</u> from earlier lessons. Then answer the comprehension questions.

Victor: Roberto, I heard you got a new job, and you're going to move!
Roberto: That's right!
Victor: Tell me about it. How did that **come about?**
Roberto: Yeah, I didn't really want to move at first, but it makes sense for the new job. If I don't move, the trip between my house and work will take about an hour each way.
Victor: That's too long.
Roberto: Plus, I found a really good place. It's nicer than my current house, and it's quieter, too.
Victor: That's good. What about the job?
Roberto: I first saw the job online six months ago. It's similar to what I do now, but it pays better, and I would be part of the management team. But, since I didn't want to move, I just kept **putting off** applying for it. Finally, after a really bad week at work, I **gave in** and <u>filled out</u> the online application and sent my resume. I got a response and an interview right away.
Victor: When was that?
Roberto: Two months ago. The interview process went quickly, and I accepted the job. I started a month ago, so right now I'm making the one-hour drive. They agreed that I could work remotely one day a week, so that saves me some gas. I spent weekends looking for a new house, and I found one two weeks ago. I'm waiting for the paperwork to <u>come through</u> now, and I'm hoping I can move in sometime next month.

Victor: Wow. Everything happened so quickly!
Roberto: It did. It's exciting, but it's a lot of change. I'm looking forward to having things <u>settle down</u>.
Victor: Are you going to be selling your house here?
Roberto: No. I'm going to rent it out because, with all the university students here, I don't think it'll be hard to find people to rent it.
Victor: Probably not, but are you going to handle all of the day-to-day problems on top of your new job?
Roberto: No, I'm actually going to hire a company to manage that for me.
Victor: Oh, that's good. Well, good luck with everything.
Roberto: Thanks.

1. What is new in Roberto's life?

    a. He has a new job.
    b. He has a new house.
    c. He has a new job and will have a new house soon.

2. How long does it take Roberto to get to his new job now?

    a. about 30 minutes
    b. about 60 minutes
    c. about 120 minutes

3. What is true about Roberto's new house?

a. It is quieter than his current house.
b. It is newer than his current house.
c. It is bigger than his current house.

4. When did Roberto start his new job?

a. one month ago
b. two months ago
c. six months ago

5. Who will live in Roberto's house after he moves?

a. Victor
b. a management company
c. renters

6. How do Victor and Roberto know each other?

a. They work together.
b. They are neighbors.
c. We do not know from this conversation.

ACTIVITY 2: LEARNING NEW PHRASAL VERBS

Read this information about 3 phrasal verbs. Study the example sentences carefully. To help learn them, read the example sentences aloud or write them on a sheet of paper or in a document.

#145: COME ABOUT

145: happen or occur, sometimes unexpectedly (Note: usually used in past tense)

- I heard that your boss left the company. How did that **come about?**
- The decision to close the factory for good **came about** after many long discussions.

#146: GIVE IN (TO)

146: stop resisting or stop fighting

- The clerk didn't want to **give in** and admit he had made a mistake, but in the end, that's exactly what he did.
- The little girl kept crying for some candy, and her dad finally **gave in to** her demands and gave her what she wanted.

#147: PUT OFF

147A: postpone

- Can we **put off** our meeting until next week?
- The rain forced us to **put off** our picnic until another time.

147B: PUT OFF (BY): cause someone to feel strong dislike for (Note: often used in passive voice with the preposition *by*)

- I was really **put off by** her bad manners. I don't want to be around her anymore.
- The high crime rate has **put off** a lot of tourists from visiting the city.

ACTIVITY 3: PRACTICING IMPORTANT PHRASES

Give the phrasal verb for the meaning. Be sure to use the correct verb tense.

1. stopped resisting = _____ _____
2. delayed washing her car = _____ _____ washing her car
3. it happened suddenly = it _____ _____ suddenly
4. was bothered by the smell = was _____ _____ _____ the smell
5. postponed the trip = _____ _____ the trip

ACTIVITY 4: USING CORRECT PREPOSITIONS

Read the sentences carefully and add the missing prepositions for each phrasal verb.

1. I keep **putting** _____ cleaning out my garage.
2. After a stressful day, she often **gives** _____ to her desire for sugar.

3. The problem **came** _____ because the schools don't have enough money.
4. He was **put** _____ _____ all the yelling at the meeting, so he left.
5. The new law **came** _____ because of all of the online crime.
6. I was so tired that I just **gave** _____ and let the dog sleep on the bed.

ACTIVITY 5: VERBS IN CONTEXT

Use the context to select the correct verb for the sentence.

1. Don't (come about, give in, put off, put off by) doing your taxes for too long.
2. Once the last person (came about, gave in, put off, put off by), everyone signed the new agreement.
3. Dad always (comes about, gives in, puts off, puts off by) and lets us have pizza on Fridays.
4. I saw that you bought a new house. How did that (come about, give in, put off, put off by)?
5. She was (come about, give in, put off, put off by) the dog's barking, so she left the shelter without a puppy.

ACTIVITY 6: ONLINE PRACTICE

You can practice the phrasal verbs from this lesson at

https://bit.ly/3DDNQtq

Here you can use *Flashcards*, *Learn*, or *Match*. You can also have more guided practice with *Q-Chat* that offers *Teach me*, *Quiz me*, and *Apply my knowledge*.

Answers for Lesson 9

Activity 1

1. c
2. b
3. a
4. a
5. c
6. c

Activity 3

1. gave in
2. put off
3. came about
4. put off by
5. put off

Activity 4

1. off
2. in
3. about
4. off by
5. about
6. in

Activity 5

1. put off
2. gave in
3. gives in
4. come about
5. put off by

LESSON 10
CLOSE DOWN; PUT IN; SET ABOUT

A food truck selling tacos

ACTIVITY 1: CONVERSATION PRACTICE

Read this conversation. Think about the meanings of the **3 new bold verbs**. Remember the meanings of the underlined verbs from earlier lessons. Then answer the comprehension questions.

Liza: Oh, no! I'm so disappointed!
Marco: What happened?
Liza: I just found out that my favorite restaurant has **closed down**. I still can't believe it. I usually go there once a week. And I was planning to go there for lunch today.
Marco: Which restaurant are you talking about?
Liza: Taqueria del Sol.
Marco: Oh, no! I loved that place too. Do you know why they closed?
Liza: No. And I was just there last week. I can't believe they didn't tell their customers this news.
Marco: There's a lot of construction in that part of town. Aren't they **putting in** a new stadium a few blocks from there?
Liza: Yeah. I thought that would help with business. I don't know what happened.
Marco: There are a lot of taco food trucks in that part of town now. Maybe there's just too much competition.
Liza: That's true. I guess I'll have to **set about** finding a new taco place where the food is just as good and affordable. I'm going to look online and see if I can find a place. I really wanted tacos today.
Marco: Tacos sound good, but we could also get pizza

or curry. My neighborhood has a good taco place, but it's too far for us to go on our lunch break.

Liza: Well, they didn't <u>take down</u> their website. That's good! It looks like Taqueria del Sol also has food trucks – and they're serving today!

Marco: Great! Maybe the restaurant was costing them too much, so they decided to just do the trucks. They can probably <u>take in</u> more money that way. What do you think?

Liza: Yeah, that makes sense.

Marco: I hope they still have my favorites on their menu. The tortilla soup is also really good.

Liza: So, according to their website, their trucks will be in three locations around lunch time, and one of them is only a few blocks from here. I'm going to go find it. I think I can make it back to work before our break ends. Do you want to come with me?

Marco: Yes, let's go! I really love their tacos!

1. Why is Liza disappointed?

    a. Her lunch break is too short.
    b. A favorite restaurant is closed.
    c. The stadium doesn't have any restaurants.

2. What happened to Taqueria del Sol?

    a. The restaurant moved.
    b. The restaurant closed.
    c. The restaurant raised its prices.

3. What does Liza like to order from Taqueria del Sol?

   a. tacos
   b. tortilla soup
   c. tacos and tortilla soup

4. What is the good news?

   a. They can still eat Taqueria del Sol's food.
   b. There will be a new stadium.
   c. The restaurant is going to re-open.

5. What are Liza and Marco going to eat for lunch?

   a. tacos
   b. pizza
   c. We do not know from this conversation.

6. What are Liza and Marco going to do next?

   a. They will find a Taqueria del Sol food truck.
   b. They will find a place to eat pizza or curry.
   c. They will go back to work without lunch.

ACTIVITY 2: LEARNING NEW PHRASAL VERBS

Read this information about 3 phrasal verbs. Study the example sentences carefully. To help learn them, read the example sentences aloud or write them on a sheet of paper or in a document.

#148. CLOSE DOWN

148: stop operations, usually related to a business

- Unfortunately, that little restaurant is going to **close down** next week.
- The city **closed down** the highway after the bridge fell.

#149. PUT IN

149A: insert or put inside a place

- First, you have to **put in** two batteries.
- I forgot to **put in** the sugar when I was making the cookies, so they don't taste very good.

149B: contribute time or effort to a project or activity

- If you **put in** just 15 minutes a day, you can learn a lot of new words.
- Everyone in our office **put in** $5 so we could buy a gift for Michael.

149C: submit a request or application (NOTE: used in work situations)

- I'm going to **put in** an application to work at that restaurant on weekends.
- Five companies **put in** proposals to win the contract to build the new school.

#150. SET ABOUT [+ VERB-ing]

150: begin some action or task with a specific purpose in mind

- After the storm, the workers **set about** repairing the roof.
- First, he **set about** making a list of all the supplies he would need.

ACTIVITY 3: PRACTICING IMPORTANT PHRASES

Give the phrasal verb for the meaning. Be sure to use the correct verb tense.

1. adding a washer and dryer = ____ ____ a washer and dryer
2. prepared a plan to paint a mural = ____ ____ painting a mural
3. contributed hours of work = ____ ____ hours of work
4. submitting a proposal = ____ ____ a proposal

5. stopped operating a business = _____ _____ a business

ACTIVITY 4: USING CORRECT PREPOSITIONS

Read the sentences carefully and add the missing prepositions for each phrasal verb.

1. I **put** _____ a lot of overtime on that project.
2. Is there still time for us to **put** _____ a bid on this construction project?
3. I heard the road **closed** _____ because of the flooding.
4. The school decided to **put** _____ a new alarm system.
5. The library branch I visit all the time is **closing** _____.
6. Can you tell me how you **set** _____ writing your book?

ACTIVITY 5: VERBS IN CONTEXT

Use the context to select the correct verb for the sentence.

1. She was excited to (close down, put in, set about) her application for the job.
2. After the election, they (closed down, put in, set about) hiring new staff.
3. Did you hear the city is (closing down, putting in, setting about) the old hospital?

4. I was (closing down, putting in, setting about) a new dishwasher when the power went out.
5. How can you just (close down, put in, set about) a major highway with no warning?

∼

ACTIVITY 6: ONLINE PRACTICE

You can practice the phrasal verbs from this lesson at

https://bit.ly/3R1A5ru

Here you can use *Flashcards*, *Learn*, or *Match*. You can also have more guided practice with *Q-Chat* that offers *Teach me*, *Quiz me*, and *Apply my knowledge*.

Answers for Lesson 10

Activity 1

1. b
2. b
3. c
4. a
5. a
6. a

Activity 3

1. putting in
2. set about
3. put in
4. putting in
5. closed down

Activity 4

1. in
2. in
3. down
4. in
5. down
6. about

Activity 5

1. put in
2. set about
3. closing down
4. putting in
5. close down

ABOUT THE PUBLISHER

Thank you for your time and attention! If you found the book useful, we hope you will leave a short review on the site where you purchased this book to let other readers know of your experience.

To be notified about new titles and special contests, events, and sales from Wayzgoose Press, please visit our website at

http://wayzgoosepress.com

and sign up for our mailing list. (We send email infrequently, and you can unsubscribe at any time.)

www.ingramcontent.com/pod-product-compliance
Lightning Source LLC
Chambersburg PA
CBHW060815050426
42449CB00008B/1668